Primarily Thinking

Grades 2 - 3

Written by
Judy Leimbach

Illustrated by
Mary Lou Johnson

First published 2005 by Prufrock Press Inc.

Published 2021 by Routledge
605 Third Avenue, New York, NY 10017
2 Park Square, Milton Park, Abingdon, Oxon OX14 4RN

Routledge is an imprint of the Taylor & Francis Group, an informa business

ISBN 13: 978-1-59363-038-6 (pbk)

Edited by Dianne Draze

Routledge
Taylor & Francis Group
NEW YORK AND LONDON

Contents

In these exercises, students are asked to look for similarities and differences between things. This skill requires attention to detail, creative and critical observation, and flexible thinking. It is an important prerequisite to classification.

In these exercises, students are asked to determine the common qualities or properties of several items. This skill allows students to deal with the world in a more global, generalized fashion rather than remembering the specific characteristics of each item.

These pages ask students to determine whether things are facts (proven and not open to dispute) or opinions (ideas that may differ from one person to another).

In these exercises students are asked to establish a relationship in which one incident causes something else to happen. This is an important concept in science, problem solving, and personal development.

These exercises have students look for repeating items or identify a relationship between members of a set such that one can predict what future members of the set will be. Looking for patterns trains the mind to think logically, to look for relationships, to make predictions, and encourages persistence and flexible thinking.

When students do sequencing exercises, they will be putting a group of things in an arrangement in such a way that there is a first, second, third, etc. component. There are many different ways of ordering groups of things (size, color, intensity, time, age, etc.). Before students can put items of each group in order, they must discover the relationship that dictates the sequence.

Information for the Instructor

Why Teach Thinking?

Good educators realize that students need more than instruction in reading, spelling and arithmetic. They recognize the need for students at all grade levels to be actively engaged in learning how to think. Mere acquisition of knowledge is not enough if our schools are to successfully prepare students for the future. In addition to being able to retrieve information, students should be able to critically analyze the information. This requires several different thinking skills. The lessons and activities in this book will help the teacher in the lower elementary grades to develop students' analytical thinking skills. These activities introduce students to various thinking skills with isolated, concrete examples and exercises. *Primarily Thinking* is a beginning — a foundation for additional thinking instruction. Once students have mastered a basic understanding of these skills, they will be able to develop the skills to a more advanced level. As students get older, they should be able to apply these same skills with more complex and abstract situations, information, problems, and concepts. Given these skills, students will be more adequately prepared to deal with life situations in a logical, rational manner than if they have only been taught to digest information and balance a checkbook. These thinking skills are crucial to thoughtful living.

Thinking and Reading

As students develop their reading skills, we need to emphasize these higher-level thought processes having to do with the relationships between ideas if we are to develop their comprehension and critical reading skills. Discerning the difference between fact and opinion is an essential component of critical reading. Sequencing activities help students see sequential relationships and to think logically. Determining cause-effect relationships is one of the skills involved in making predictions. Understanding of classifications or categories is a prerequisite for understanding main idea and supporting details.

Using This Book

Analytical ability is an important component of critical thinking. This book provides practice in the breakdown of material into its constituent parts as students compare attributes, discern differences, detect relationships, and observe the way things are organized. Students are introduced to the thinking skills that will allow them to compare and contrast, classify, distinguish between facts and opinions, identify cause and effect, recognize patterns, and order things in a sequential manner. Some of the activities promote divergent thinking as well as critical thinking, as students share their ideas.

The activity pages in this book can and should be used in a variety of ways. The teacher may wish to use some as individual exercises, while others may be made into overhead transparencies and used with a whole class or small group of students. In addition to the student activity pages, each section has a page of Additional Suggested Activities for the teacher to use in extending the skills taught.

Name_____

1. Underline the things that are true for oranges.

orange colored
green colored
people eat it
fruit
vegetable
grows on a tree
needs water and sunshine
can buy in a food store
has vitamins

2. Underline the things that are true for broccoli.

orange colored
green colored
people eat it
fruit
vegetable
grows on a tree
needs water and sunshine
can buy in a food store
has vitamins

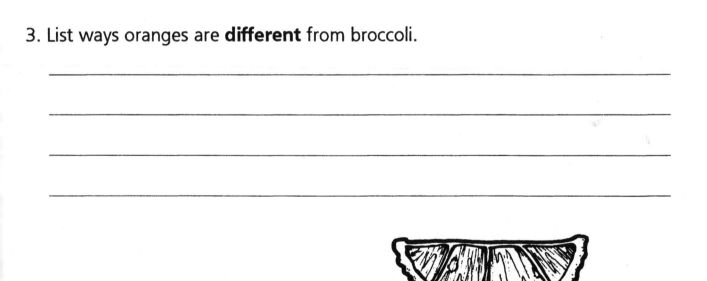

3. List ways oranges are **different** from broccoli.

_____

_____

_____

_____

4. List ways oranges are **similar** to broccoli.

_____

_____

_____

_____

Name_____

1. List things that describe or are true for a puppy.

List things that describe or are true for a young child.

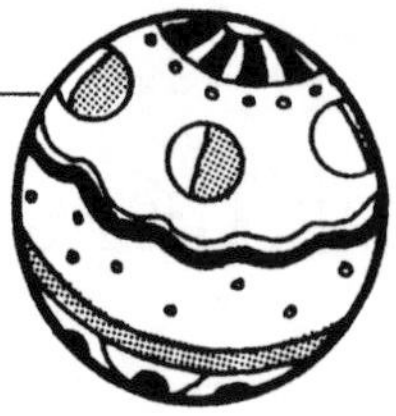

_____   _____

_____   _____

_____   _____

_____   _____

_____   _____

2. How is a young child like a puppy?

_____

_____

_____

3. How is a puppy different from a young child?

_____

_____

_____

Name_____

The things in each pair below are different, but they are also alike in many ways. Think of at least three ways each pair is **alike**.

1. _____

   _____

   _____

   _____

Piano

Guitar

2. _____

   _____

   _____

Roller Skate

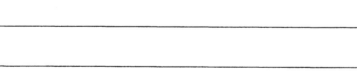

Train

3. _____

   _____

   _____

Mitten

Boot

Name_____

The following pairs of things are alike in some ways and different in some ways. For each pair, write three ways they are **different.**

1. pen   pencil

_____

_____

_____

2. baseball marble

_____

_____

3. truck   car

_____

_____

_____

4. rose   dandelion

_____

_____

_____

Name_____

1. Cardinals and bald eagles are both birds, so they are similar in many ways. List five ways cardinals and bald eagles are **alike.**

_____

_____

_____

_____

_____

2. There are many differences between a cardinal and a bald eagle. Mark each phrase below with a **C** or an **E** to show whether it is true of a cardinal or a bald eagle.

_____Male is bright red

_____Eats small animals like rodents and fish

_____Eats seeds

_____Is a symbol for the United States

_____Builds a nest large enough for a man to fit in

_____Is a songbird

_____Head is covered with white feathers

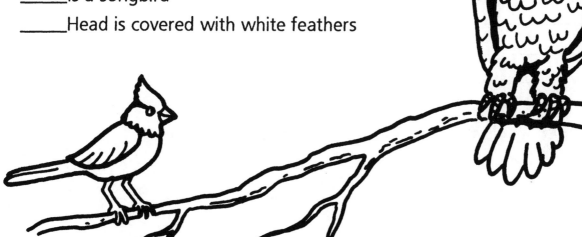

Name_____

Even though a bat flies, it is not a bird. Compare a bat to a hummingbird. Think of three ways they are alike and different.

1. A bat is **like** a hummingbird because...

a._____

b._____

c._____

2. A bat is **different** from a hummingbird because...

a._____

b._____

c._____

Even though a penguin does not fly, it is a bird. Compare a penguin to a hummingbird. Think of three ways they are alike and different.

3. A penguin is **like** a hummingbird because...

a._____

b._____

c._____

4. A penguin is **different** from a hummingbird because...

a._____

b._____

c._____

Name_____

Choose a friend to compare with yourself.

1. Your friend's name _____

2. In what ways are you and your friend **alike**?

_____

_____

_____

_____

_____

3. In what ways are you and your friend **different**?

_____

_____

_____

_____

_____

4. On the back of this piece of paper draw a picture of you and your friend.

Additional Comparison Activities

1. Give students practice in analyzing attributes by having them compare two similar items, naming the similarities and then the differences. For example; display two stuffed animals. Ask students to share ideas about how the two are alike, then how they are different. Other examples might be two kinds of plants, a pen and a pencil, a watch and a clock, two different articles of clothing, a car and a train, a baseball and a basketball, a thermometer and a ruler.

2. Stretch student's creative thinking as well as analytical thinking by having them think of ways dissimilar things are alike. For example; Ask "How is a baby like a banana?" Answers might be both are small, both begin with "ba", both can get smelly, a banana grows on a tree and a baby is part of a family tree, both are soft, and both have skin.

3. Cut out pictures of a wide variety of things from magazines and catalogs. Mount the pictures on 4" x 6" index cards. Have students randomly draw cards and then compare and contrast the items pictured.

4. Compare stories of the same genre (fables, fairy tales, realistic fiction, fantasy, etc.) read in class. For example; compare the two fables, "The Lion and the Mouse" and "The Fox and the Crow". Similarities might be both are short stories, both have animals for the main characters, the animals do not have names, there is conversation between the animals and both teach a lesson.

5. From your school or local library check out a variety of alphabet books. Have students read and analyze them, comparing attributes. They may keep a reading record where they record the titles of books read and list their characteristics.

6. Using attribute blocks have students compare them for similarities and differences. Have students build difference trains by placing one attribute block on the desk and then make a line of blocks where each of the following blocks differs from the preceding block in a specified number of ways, (one, two, three, or four differences). For example, one-difference trains will have three attributes that are the same and only one attribute that is different.

7. Have students compare two characters from stories they are reading. The characters could both be from the same story or could be characters with similar roles in different stories (like Cinderella and Snow White). Have students list attributes of each character and then compare and contrast the attributes. Encourage creative perspectives.

Name_____

We classify things or put things into groups because they are alike in some way. In each box below are things that are alike in some way. Find how they are alike and label each group.

1.

Group name _____

2.

Group name _____

3.

Group name_____

4.

Group name _____

5.

Group name_____

6.

Group name _____

Name_____

Match each group with one of the descriptions in the box. Write the letter of the description next to the number of the correct group. Add one more thing to each group.

```
a. things that fly          e. yellow things
b. hard things              f. ways to get information
c. things to play with      g. things to write with
d. tools                    h. kinds of animals
```

1._____ball, jump rope, skateboard,_____

2._____chalk, pencil, crayon,_____

3._____lemon, dandelion, banana,_____

4._____rock, wood, glass,_____

5._____butterfly, airplane, bird,_____

6._____bird, mammal, reptile,_____

7._____newspaper, television, radio,_____

8._____hammer, pliers, screwdriver,_____

Name_____

Cut out these things. Arrange them in groups so that things in the group are similar. Paste them on a piece of paper. Label the groups.

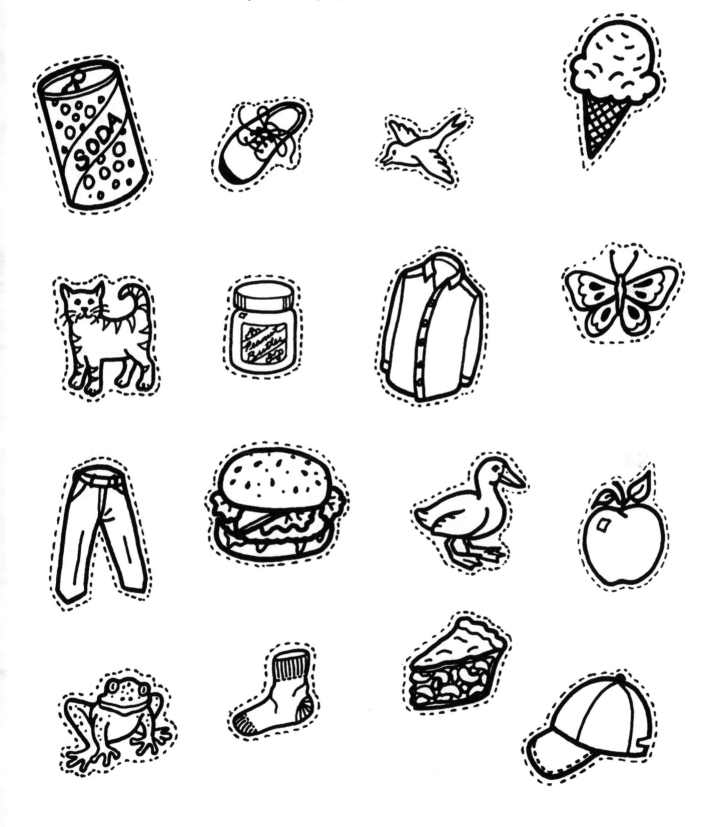

Name_____

1. The words in the box below can be sorted into three groups — rooms, furniture and shelters. Write each word in the proper group in the chart below.

house	living room	trailer	chair
kitchen	couch	bedroom	tent
table	apartment	bathroom	desk

rooms	**furniture**	**shelters**
_____	_____	_____
_____	_____	_____
_____	_____	_____
_____	_____	_____

2. The words in the box below name things people wear. Sort them into groups.

shirt	hat	bracelet	blouse
ring	necklace	dress	boots
gloves	skirt	scarf	earrings

jewelry	**outdoor clothing**	**other clothing**
_____	_____	_____
_____	_____	_____
_____	_____	_____
_____	_____	_____

Name_____

1. Look at the words in the box below. Think of a way to sort them into two groups. Write the names of the groups on the labels at the top of each list in the chart below. Then write each word in the correct group in your chart.

| cow | horse | calf | colt |
| chick | bear | cub | hen |

_____	_____
_____	_____
_____	_____
_____	_____

2. Think of a way to sort the words in this box into two groups. Label the groups and write the words in the correct places in the chart.

| flower | reptile | tree | bird |
| mammal | vine | bush | fish |

_____	_____
_____	_____
_____	_____

Name_____

Here are some things that can be grouped together. One thing in each line does not belong to the group. Cross out the thing that does not belong.

1.

2.

3.

4. bean, carrot, apple, pea, squash

5. George, James, Greg, Bill, Carol

6. hammer, eraser, pliers, wrench, screwdriver

7. spoon, knife, saw, scissors, razor blade

8. magazine, book, newspaper, television, letter

9. sandal, boot, glove, tennis shoe, slipper

10. 10, 15, twenty, 25, 30

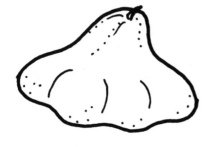

Name_____

Sort the numbers in the box into different groups. You may put some numbers into more than one group.

10	2	9	30	5
14	49	1	18	50
90	8	20	33	7
45	70	55	12	100

1. Even numbers	2. Numbers you say when you count by fives
3. Numbers between 20 and 50	4. Numbers that have zero ones
5. Two-digit numbers	6. Odd numbers

Name_____

Each box is labeled with the kinds of things that go in it. Think of three or more things that could go in each box. List them in the boxes.

1. things with wheels,
   but no motor.

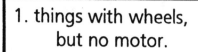

2. things you eat with a spoon

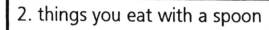

3. wooden things
   in a classroom

4. things filled with air

5. long, thin things

6. things you peel

Additional Classification Activities

1. Ask students to name common attributes of things in a group. For example:
   robin, blue jay, woodpecker   milk, salt, snow
   squirrel, racoon, beaver   lion, tiger, leopard
   car, bus, truck   grass, limes, peas

2. Call on several students who share a particular attribute to form a group. Call on others who do not share the attribute to stand outside the group. Have other students name the group. For example, students wearing glasses, velcro shoes, short sleeves, buttons on shirt or blouse.

3. Play a "yes" and "no" game. List things under "yes" that belong together in some way, things under "no" that would not fit in the group. Have students analyze the list and determine what attribute(s) is necessary for something to go into the "yes" group. Students who figure it out can give other examples of things that would fit into the "yes" group. Other students can name things and as the teacher writes them under "yes" or "no" they can continue to analyze the groups. An example, for double letters would be:

Yes	No
books	pages
mittens	gloves
trees	leaves
puppies	dogs

4. Play **"Name the Category"** game with partners or groups. One person is shown the category name. That person has to get his/her partner or the group to name the category by naming things that would go in the category. For example:
   category - *things with zippers*
   possible clues - *jacket, boots, pants, purse*
   category - *things you say on the telephone*
   possible clues - *Hello, She's not home, May I take a message?, You have the wrong number*

5. Use attribute blocks or other manipulatives to form sets for students to analyze. Place items with common attributes inside a loop, others outside. Have students analyze to determine the necessary attribute for set membership. Advance to two overlapping loops and intersecting sets.

 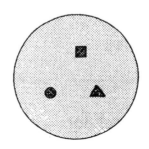 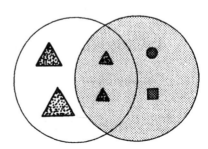

Fill in the blanks to make true statements. These true statements are facts.

1. I am _____years old.

2. I go to_____School.

3. Check the statements below that you agree with.

_____Most children watch too much television.
_____The best part of school is math class.
_____Summer is the best time of the year.
_____The best part of school is recess.
_____Watching television is boring.
_____Watching television is fun.
_____Baseball is an exciting game.
_____Ice cream is yummy.
_____Spinach is yummy.
_____School is fun.

The statements you checked are statements you agree with, but they are not facts — they are opinions. A **fact** is something that can be tested by observing, counting, or measuring. It can be shown that it is either true or false. An **opinion** is a statement that cannot be proven to be true or false. You can only agree or disagree with it. One person may agree with the statement, but others may disagree.

4. Write a fact about your school.

_____

5. Write an opinion about your school.

_____

Name_____

Compare your opinions with other people's opinions. Think about what is your favorite television show and your favorite ice cream flavor. Ask five other people these same questions and write their answers below.

favorite television show   favorite ice cream flavor

_____   _____

_____   _____

_____   _____

_____   _____

_____   _____

Did some people agree with you? Was there anything that all the people agreed upon? Sometimes many people have the same opinion, but that still doesn't make it a fact. Even if everyone in your class chose chocolate ice cream as the best flavor, someone else might still disagree. Therefore, it is an opinion, not a fact.

Here are some statements about food. Put an **F** in front of the ones that are facts and an **O** in front of the ones that are opinions.

____1. Peas are vegetables.

____2. Carrots are orange.

____3. Beans are better than peas or carrots.

____4. All vegetables are yucky.

____5. Apples are not vegetables.

____6. Red apples are better than green apples.

____7. Peas grow in a pod.

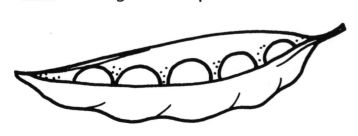

Name_____

Some of the sentences below are facts. Some of them are opinions. Mark each with an **F** or an **O** to show whether it is a fact or an opinion.

_____1. California is the best state in the United States.

_____2. Disney World is in Orlando, Florida.

_____3. There are fifty states in the United States.

_____4. Carrots are delicious.

_____5. Carrots are a vegetable.

_____6. Whales are not fish.

_____7. Riding a roller coaster is scary.

_____8. Dogs make better pets than fish.

_____9. Fish breathe through their gills.

_____10. Disney World is a great place to go on your vacation.

_____11. Two nickels are worth as much as a dime.

_____12. Flowers are pretty.

_____13. There are twelve eggs in a dozen.

_____14. Fried eggs taste better than scrambled eggs.

Name_____

Mark each sentence with an **F** if it is a fact and with an **O** if it is an opinion.

_____1. There are three fielders in the outfield.

_____2. Boys are better baseball players than girls.

_____3. The pitcher is the most important player on the team.

_____4. There are nine innings in a regular game.

_____5. Three strikes make an out.

_____6. Oakland has the best baseball team.

_____7. Football is more exciting to watch than baseball.

_____8. Each team gets three outs in an inning.

_____9. When the batter hits a home run, every player on base scores.

_____10. Playing baseball is fun.

_____11. Seeing a baseball game at the ball park is better than watching it on television.

Write three baseball opinions of your own.

12. _____

13. _____

14. _____

For each of the things below, write one fact and one opinion.

1. Name a food _____

    fact _____

    _____

    opinion _____

    _____

2. Name a television program _____

  fact _____

_____

opinion _____

_____

3. Name a sport _____

  fact _____

_____

opinion _____

_____

4. Name a famous person _____

    fact _____

    _____

    opinion _____

    _____

Name_____

The paragraph below contains many facts about giraffes. There are some opinions mixed in with the facts. Draw a line under the sentences that are opinions.

Giraffes are the most interesting animals in the zoo. They are the tallest of the land animals. Their long legs and long necks allow them to eat leaves off of trees as high as fifteen feet above ground. It is fun to watch them eat. They wrap their long tongues around a branch and strip the leaves off. Their black tongues are funny looking! Baby giraffes may be more than five feet tall when they are born. They are beautiful animals.

Choose another animal. Write a fact and an opinion about this animal.

animal _____

fact _____

_____

_____

opinion _____

_____

_____

Name_____

The newspaper items below contain some facts and some opinions. Draw a red line under all the opinions.

$2.00 Off Coupon
The Chicken Coop
Best Fried Chicken in the U.S.A.
This coupon is worth **$2.00 off** any bill over $10.00 Monday through Thursday - Expires December 31
You'll love our chicken!!

For Sale:

Cocker Spaniel puppies.
12 weeks old - $50.00 each.
Will make wonderful pets.

Apartment for Rent

3 room apartment,
reasonable price.
good location,
beautiful cozy rooms.
Call: (555) 555-5555

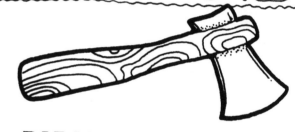

PARAMOUNT THEATER

"The Big Story"

Starring **Paul B. Unyon**

The most exciting adventure story of the year!!

Vote for I. M. Honest for U.S. Senator

Our state needs a man like **I. M. Honest**.
He will be the best Senator ever to represent our state in Congress.

Vote on Election Day!!

Name_____

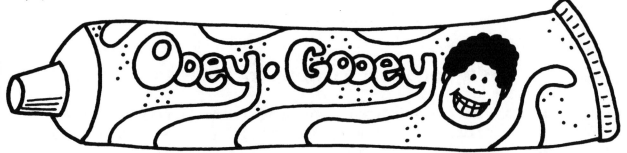

Design a magazine advertisement for Ooey-Gooey Toothpaste. Include at least two facts and at least two opinions in your ad.

Additional Fact/Opinion Activities

1. Give each student an index card. Print a large F on one side and an O on the other. As you make statements to the class have them hold up the F side if they think a statement is a fact and the O side if they think it is an opinion.

2. Hold up an object or a picture for all students to observe. Have students make factual statements about the item, then give opinions about it.

3. After reading a non-fiction book or seeing an educational movie or videotape, ask students to recall some of the facts they learned. Then discuss the students' opinions of the book, movie, or video.

4. Have students make a poster advertising a favorite book. The poster should display at least one fact and one opinion about the book.

5. Have students write a book review. The first paragraph should contain factual information and the second paragraph should state opinions.

6. Have students bring in examples of advertisements that contain some facts and some opinions. Display these ads and have the class analyze them and distinguish between the facts and opinions.

7. Discuss how widely shared opinions are often thought of as facts. Widely shared opinions may become values, but they are not facts. For example: "Dogs are not good to eat" may be thought of as a fact by many because most people in our culture share that opinion; however, in some other cultures this may not be the case.

Name_____

Sometimes things that happen cause other things to happen. For example, if you stick a pin into a balloon, that will cause the balloon to pop.

Sticking the pin in is the **cause**. The pop is the **effect**.

The <u>cause</u> in each happening below is underlined. Identify the effect by drawing a box around it.

1. When <u>the mailman comes to the door,</u> the dog barks.

2. The <u>sun came out,</u> and the snowman began to melt.

3. Sarah cried because her <u>snowman melted.</u>

4. Michelle was worried because <u>she forgot to do her homework.</u>

5. <u>The tide came in</u> and washed the sand castle away.

6. <u>Laura spilled her milk</u> and got her new dress all wet.

7. Erik's bobber went down quickly when <u>a big fish swallowed his hook.</u>

8. Paul was a big hero when <u>his home run won the game.</u>

9. <u>Josh bumped Melissa</u> and made her drop her lunch.

Name_____

Match each cause with the most likely effect.

Cause

1._____Tricia's alarm clock broke.

2._____A car ran over a nail.

3._____It rained.

4._____The sun came out.

5._____A glass slipped out of her hand.

6._____The music stopped.

7._____He forgot to fill his car with gas.

8._____It didn't rain for five months.

9._____Jason didn't do his homework.

10._____The team won the game.

Effect

a. He got a bad grade.

b. It dried up all the rain.

c. It broke in many pieces.

d. The car stopped running.

e. She was late for school.

f. The grass turned brown.

g. The boys could not play outside.

h. The dancers stopped dancing.

i. They were very happy.

j. Its tire went flat.

Sometimes one effect could have several possible causes. Write two possible causes for each of the effects below.

Possible Cause   **Effect**

1. _____   Pat was crying.
   _____

2. _____   The grass was wet.
   _____

3. _____   The crowd was cheering.
   _____

4. _____   Meredith was surprised.
   _____

5. _____   The children walked outside quickly.
   _____

Name_____

Often something that happens will have several possible effects. For instance:

Cause
The pencil broke.

Possible Effects
1. Bill couldn't do his homework.
2. Bill has to buy a new pencil.

For each happening below, write two possible effects.

1. Tricia overslept.   a. _____

                            b. _____

2. Jean didn't do her homework. a. _____

                            b. _____

3. Paul's team won the game.   a. _____

                            b. _____

4. James had a birthday party. a. _____

                            b. _____

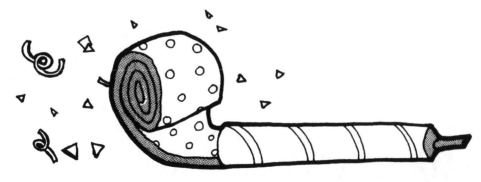

Name_____

Think of two possible causes for each effect below.

Possible Causes	**Effect**

1. _____ The dog began to bark loudly.

_____

2. _____ Mrs. Brown was proud of Richard.

_____

3. _____ Everyone laughed.

Think of two possible effects for each of the phrases below.

Cause	**Possible Effects**

4. Ron missed the bus.   _____

_____

5. The telephone rang.   _____

_____

Name_____

Look at each picture below, then write a cause and effect sentence to go with each picture. Underline the <u>cause</u> once and the <u>effect</u> twice.

The snowman began melting when <u>the sun came ou</u>

_____
_____

_____
_____

_____
_____

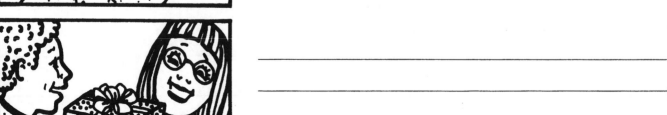

_____
_____

Name_____

Look at everything that is happening in this picture. Write five cause and effect sentences about the picture. Each sentence should tell about something that happened (the effect) and what caused it to happen (the cause).

1. _____

_____

2. _____

_____

3. _____

_____

4. _____

_____

5. _____

_____

Name_____

Match each effect below with the most logical cause. Put the correct number on the line in front of the effect.

Causes

1. The clown did funny tricks.

2. It got colder.

3. Dan didn't get enough sleep.

4. The umpire called "strike three."

5. Charles forgot the food in the oven.

6. The pile of leaves burned.

7. Jill rang the bell.

8. Mike used too much soap.

9. The bat hit the ball.

10. Lisa disobeyed her parents.

Effects

a._____She got in trouble.

b._____The food burned.

c._____The air was filled with smoke.

d._____Liz put on a sweater.

e._____Everyone laughed.

f._____A sound rang through the room.

g._____David was called out.

h._____He was tired.

i._____The ball sailed through the air.

j._____He had too many bubbles.

Name_____

Our behavior often has an effect on other people. Some things we do have a good or positive effect on others. Some things we do have a bad or negative effect on others.

Put a **+** sign by each behavior that you think would have a positive (good) effect on other people. Put a **-** sign by each behavior that you think would have a negative (bad) effect on others.

1._____being selfish

2._____lying to people

3._____helping others

4._____being a good sport

5._____cheating in a game

6._____making a gift for someone

7._____always being willing to share

8._____always trying to be first

9._____taking turns without complaining

10._____teasing someone who lost a race

11._____congratulating the winning team

12._____praising someone for what they have done

13._____laughing at someone who made a mistake

14._____taking something that does not belong to you

15._____thanking someone for something he or she has done

16._____bragging when you've done better than someone else

Name_____

Here is a list of events. The first event caused the second event to happen. The second event made the third event happen, and so on. Number the events to show how each one caused the next event.

__1__ Jill kicked the bucket.

_____ The cat jumped.

__6__ She yelled "Ouch!"

_____ The bird fell off its perch.

_____ The bucket fell over.

_____ Jill slipped and fell on the water.

_____ The cat scared the bird.

_____ She hurt her leg when she fell.

_____ Her yell scared the cat.

_____ All the water spilled out of the bucket.

Write two events that could either come before or after this chain of events.

_____

_____

Additional Cause/Effect Activities

1. Have students orally give probable causes for hypothetical events. For example:
   James was crying on the playground.
   The teacher was upset with Laura.
   The class had a party at school.

2. Ask students to orally give probable effects for hypothetical events. For example:
   Twelve inches of snow fell overnight.
   Sally did not clean her room when she was supposed to.
   Ben hid his little brother's toy.

3. Ask students to orally give a possible cause and possible effect for a hypothetical event. For example:
   Paul gave Erik a present.
   Mother took Kathy to the doctor.
   Maria was angry at her best friend.

4. Discuss cause/effect relationships that occur in stories students read in class.

5. Discuss cause/effect relationships in science observations and experiments done in class.

6. In problem solving, think of possible causes of the problem. This may help generate ideas for possible solutions. In evaluating ideas, list possible positive and negative effects.

7. Discuss cause/effect relationships when discussing class rules and when dealing with student behavior. Help students become more aware of the effects of their own behavior on themselves and others.

Name _____

A pattern is a design or a group of things that repeats. These are patterns.

 abcabcabc

These are not patterns.

 acjbkzxcd

Which of these are patterns? Circle the patterns.

1.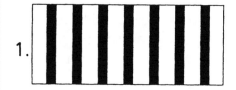

5.

2. 🔲 ◯ △ 🔲 ◯ △

6.

3. abbzzgrro

7.

4.

8.

Look for a repeating pattern in each row below. Continue the pattern by adding three more things.

1.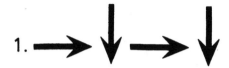

2.

3.

4.

5.

6.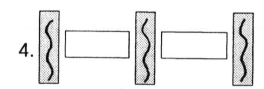

7.

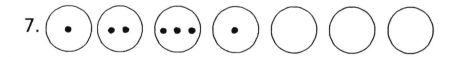

1. Continue this pattern.

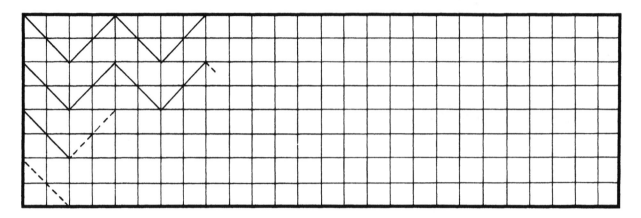

2. Continue this pattern.

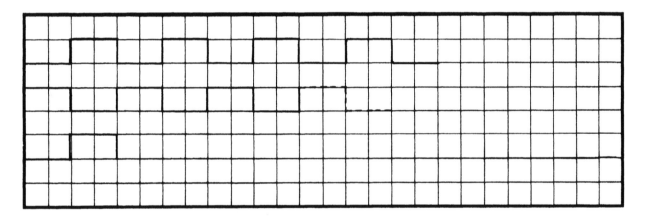

3. Continue this pattern.

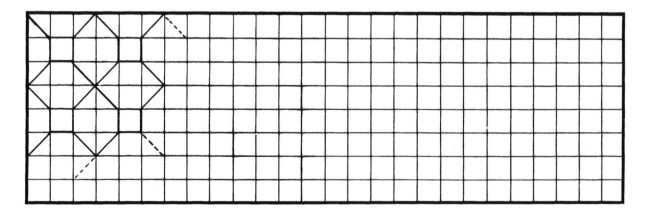

Name_____

1. Make a pattern using these shapes.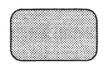

2. Make a pattern using your initials.

3. Make a pattern using arrows.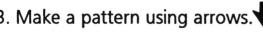

4. Create a pattern to decorate the top of a sheet of paper.

Name_____

Look for a repeating pattern in each row. Fill in the blanks with words, letters or numbers that will continue the pattern.

1. a, bb, ccc, a, _____, ccc, _____, _____, _____

2. white, black, black, white, black, _____, _____, black

3. white, gray, black, gray, white, gray, _____, _____, _____

4. at, bat, it, kit, an, _____, _____, pup, _____, son

5. apple, carrot, cherry, bean, _____, broccoli, _____, _____

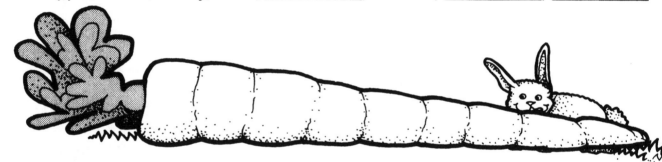

6. Lori, Sara, Louise, Suzi, Lynn, _____, _____

7. Judy, John, Melissa, Mike, Amber, _____, _____, Larry

8. hop, hopping, jump, jumping, skip, _____, _____, looking

9. a, 1, b, 2, c, 3, d, _____, _____, _____, f, _____

10. January, Monday, February, Tuesday, March, _____, _____

11. boy, boys, mouse, mice, dish, dishes, child, _____, _____, men

Name_____

Continue these patterns by adding three more things or filling in the missing parts.

1. ● ● ● ○ ● ● ● ○ ○ ○ ○ ○ ○ ○

2. snap - clap - tap - _____ - _____ - tap - snap - clap

3. ▢ ○ △ ▢ ○ △

4. ◼ ▢ ▢ ▢ ◼ ▢ ▢ ▢ ▢ ▢

5. △ ⊙ △ ⊙ △ ⊙ △

6. 5, 10, 15, 20, 5, _____, _____, 20, _____, _____

7. abc, lmn, xyz, _____, lmn, _____, _____,

8. a, 10, b, 20, c, 30, d, ____, ____, ____

Make your own pattern using symbols, letters or numbers.

9.

The notes below make rhythmic patterns.

Draw in the next four notes to continue the pattern in each line.

1.

2.

3.

4.

5.

Fill in the squares to continue each pattern.

6.

7.

8.

9.

10.

Name_____

Some patterns repeat. These are patterns like A B C A B C. Some patterns don't repeat, but there is a connection or pattern between one thing and the next thing in the group.

For example: **A C E G I**

Rule: skip a letter

Here are some patterns using numbers and letters. Look for the pattern or the rule that is used to make the pattern. Then fill in the blanks to continue the pattern.

1. 5, 10, 15, 20, 25, _____, _____, _____

2. 1, 3, 5, 7, 9, _____, _____, _____

3. 1, 11, 21, 2, 12, 22, 3, 13, _____, _____, _____

4. A, B, B, C, D, D, E, _____, _____, _____

5. 1, 10, 2, 20, 3, 30, _____, _____, _____

6. 20, 18, 16, 14, 12, _____, _____, _____

7. 8, 12, 16, 20, 24, _____, _____, _____

8. 95, 90, 85, 80, 75, _____, _____, _____

9. Alan, Bob, Carlos, Dan, Ed, _____, _____, _____

Fill in the missing numbers or letters in each chart. If the rule is not given, write the rule.

1. Rule: add 2

1	2	3	5	6	7	9
3	4					

2. Rule: double the number

1	2	3	4	5	6	7
2	4	6				

3. Rule: double the number and add 1

1	2	3	5	7	8	10
3	5	7				

4. Rule: _____

a	b	c	d	e	f	p
c	d	e				

5. Rule: _____

1	2	4	5	7	10	26
a	b	d				

Additional Pattern Activities

1. Have students observe things in the room that have patterns. For example:
   stripes on a flag
   patterns on clothing
   border design patterns
   tile patterns

2. Compare types of repeating patterns. For example:
   A B A B A B   A B C A B C
   A B B A B B   A B B C A B B C
   A B B C C A B B C C   A A B B C C A A B B C C

3. Have students use manipulatives to demonstrate various types of repeating patterns.

4. Have students use attribute blocks or other manipulatives to set up patterns for other students to analyze and try to continue the pattern.

5. Have students listen to rhythm patterns and then continue the pattern. For example:
   tap foot, clap hands, tap foot, clap hands
   snap fingers, clap, clap, snap fingers, clap, clap
   snap, snap, clap, clap, clap, snap, snap, clap, clap, clap

6. Ask individual students to devise rhythmic patterns and have classmates follow.

7. Provide students with various different kinds of rubber stamps and different colors of ink pads. Have each student select several designs and create a patterned design using the stamps.

8. Give students pieces of grid paper with one-inch squares. Have them write their names in large block letters, one letter per square. They should continue filling the squares by writing their name over and over again. When they have filled all squares of the grid with the letters of their names, have them choose a color or design for each letter of their name and lightly color each square of the grid containing that letter the chosen color.

9. Look for number patterns in counting (2, 4, 6, 8, 10, etc.). Also look for number patterns on a number chart.

```
 0   1   2   3   4   5   6   7   8   9
10  11  12  13  14  15  16  17  18  19
20  21  22  23  24  25  26  27  28  29
30  31  32  33  34  35  36  37  38  39
```

A sequence is a group of things that follow one after another in some kind of order. There are many different ways you can put things in order. These things are all in sequential order. Match each group of things with the rule that explains its order.

___1.   a. add a letter

___2.   b. add 2

___3. 2, 4, 6, 8   c. get bigger

___4. a, b, c, d, e, f,   d. alphabetical order

___5. a, at, cat, chat, cheat,   e. add details

___6.    f. subtract one

___7.    g. get darker

Name_____

Number the drawings in each row to show which should come first, second, third and fourth.

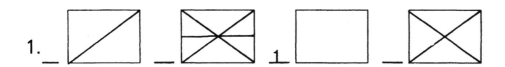

1.

2.

3.

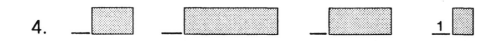

4.

5. ____important.   ____is   ____very   _1_Order

Draw the missing object in these sequences.

6.

7.

8.

Name_____

Sequencing means putting things in a logical order. Below are some things that can be put in order. Number each word to show the correct order.

1. smallest to largest

___squirrel

___horse

___ant

___mouse

___elephant

2. alphabetical order

_____Kansas

_____Alabama

_____Georgia

_____Wyoming

_____Indiana

3. oldest to youngest

___teenager

___kindergartner

___baby

___adult

___pre-schooler

4. time order

_____June

_____August

_____April

_____March

_____May

Name_____

Look at the sequences below. Draw the missing figure in each sequence.

1.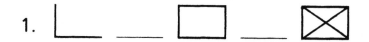

2.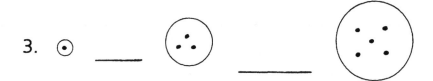

3.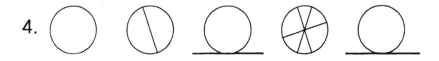

4.

5.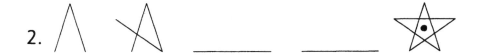

6.

7.

Name_____

1. Write these numbers in order from smallest to largest.

540, 45, 405, 54, 504, 450

_____

2. Write these measurements in order from least to greatest.

1 foot, 1 mile, 1 yard, 2 yards, 1 inch

_____

_____

3. Write these dates in order of when they occurred.

January 1, 1991   July 4, 1990
February 2, 1991   October 31, 1990

_____

_____

4. Write these in order to show size, beginning with the smallest.

state, city, country, neighborhood, house

_____

_____

5. Write these in order beginning with the shortest measurements of time.

year, second, day, minute, month, hour

_____

_____

Name_____

Number the sentences in each section in logical sequence according to the order in which they happened.

1. _____ Laura's dog wanted to go outside.

   _____ She took her dog for a walk.

   _____ Laura put the leash on him.

2. _____ She brushed her teeth.

   _____ She got out of bed.

   _____ Tiffany woke up at 8:00 a.m.

3. _____ A little chicken came out.

   _____ The hen laid an egg.

   _____ The shell cracked open.

   _____ She sat on her nest and kept it warm.

4. _____ Mother put the cookies in the oven.

   _____ Mother decided to bake some cookies.

   _____ She mixed the dough.

   _____ She got out all the ingredients.

   _____ She put the cookies on a cookie sheet to bake.

Name_____

Make a sandwich by listing the ingredients in alphabetical order.

ingredients	alphabetical order
cheese	_____
tomato	_____
ham	_____
bread	_____
onion	_____
mayonnaise	_____
lettuce	_____
pickle	_____

The sentences below tell how to really make a sandwich, but they are out of order. Number them so they are in the correct order for making a sandwich.

_____ Take a bite!

_____ Open the mayonnaise jar.

_____ Put the second slice of bread on top.

__1__ Take the ingredients out of the refrigerator.

_____ Get a sharp knife and cut it in half.

_____ Take two slices of bread out of the package.

_____ Spread mayonnaise on both slices of bread.

__5__ Stack the ham and cheese on one slice of the bread.

_____ Add lettuce, pickle, onions and tomato on top of the meat and cheese.

Name_____

The sentences below tell about one night when Trevor's family had pizza for dinner, but they are all mixed up. Number the sentences so they make sense and show the order in which things happened.

_____ Then she called and ordered a large cheese and pepperoni pizza.

_____ Trevor and his parents shared the delicious pizza.

_____ He said, "Let's order a pizza!"

_____ Then he brought the package into the kitchen.

_____ When Trevor opened the door he saw the delivery man with their pizza.

__1__ Trevor's mother asked him what he would like for dinner.

_____ His mother thought that was a good idea.

_____ He paid the delivery man.

_____ She got the phone book to look up the number for Pacci's Pizza.

__6__ After 30 minutes the doorbell rang.

Chronological order means "time order" or the order in which things happened. The sentences below tell the story of Sally and her garden, but the order is mixed up. Number the sentences in each group in the order they would have happened.

1. __**3**__ Then she dug up that section and got it ready for planting.

_____ She went out into her yard and chose a good spot for it.

_____ Sally decided she would like to plant a vegetable garden.

2. _____ She was so excited when she saw the first tiny plants appear.

_____ She planted bean seeds in her garden.

_____ Every day Sally watered her garden, waiting for the seeds to sprout.

3. _____ She took them to the house and washed them.

_____ At last it was time to pick the first beans from the garden.

_____ All during the weeks that followed Sally watered the plants and watched them grow.

4. _____ Mother cooked the beans and served them to the whole family.

_____ Everyone agreed they were delicious!

_____ She asked Mother if they could have fresh green beans for dinner.

Now read all twelve sentences in the order you numbered each group. They should tell the story of Sally's garden in correct chronological order.

Name_____

The sentences below all tell about a ski trip. Before numbering them in chronological order, group them in the following way:

Group A - happened before arriving at the ski park

Group B - happened after arriving, but before going down the hill

Group C - happened while going down the slope

After you have labeled the sentences A, B or C, number them from 1 - 10 in the order in which they happened.

group   **order**
(ABC)   (1-10)

B   **3** When they got there, he was the first to get his boots and skis on.

____ ____Finally it was his turn to get on the chairlift.

____ ____Halfway down the hill his skis hit an icy spot.

____ ____Bob was getting excited as the family packed the car for the ski trip.

____ ____His excitement grew as they drove to the ski slope.

____ ____When the chair reached the top, he jumped out and skied away.

____ ____His skis flew out from under him and down he fell!

____ ____The chair lifted him from the ground and carried him up the hill.

____ ____He waited in the chairlift line for his first trip up the hill.

C   **8** Soon he was on his way down the slope.

ooops!

The sentences below tell about one day in the life of a young boy. First group the sentences by whether they happened at home (A), on the way to school (B), at school (C), or after school (D). Then number the sentences to show the order in which they happened.

Group   Order
(ABCD)   (1-12)

____ ____ After I got dressed and ate breakfast, I left for school.

____ ____ When we got to school the first bell had already rung.

_A_ _1_ When I woke up this morning, I thought it was Saturday.

____ ____ After school we played baseball and our team won.

____ ____ On the way to school I met my friends and we walked together.

____ ____ As I walked home I thought to myself, "I think I'll watch cartoons tomorrow morning!"

____ ____ I got up and went down to watch cartoons.

____ ____ Then Mom told me it was Friday.

_C_ _8_ So we went right in.

____ ____ The day went pretty fast and soon I was on my way home.

____ ____ So I had to go back upstairs and get ready for school.

____ ____ We had reading, spelling and math in the morning.

Additional Sequencing Activities

1. Brainstorm examples of when sequence is important. Examples might be spelling words, following a recipe, building a house or giving directions.

2. Have students line up in various sequential orders; for example, by height, alphabetical order, by birthdays.

3. Discuss why alphabetical sequence is so helpful. List examples of use of alphabetical order — telephone directory, dictionary entries, card catalog, encyclopedia, index, class lists, bookshelves in the library.

4. Cut apart the boxes of a comic strip. Have students arrange them in sequential order.

5. Write main ideas of a known story on sentence strips. Have students arrange them in the order in which they occurred in the story.

6. After reading a short story to the class, have students list main events in sequence.

7. Have students give oral sequential directions for performing a specific task; for example, cutting out a heart shape, making a peanut butter and jelly sandwich, getting from your classroom to the office, figuring out the answer to a math problem, or decorating a Christmas tree.

8. Have students plan a day, listing the things they would do in chronological order.

Answers

On exercises where students' answers will vary, answers are not given in this section.

Page 5
1. orange colored
   people eat it
   fruit
   grows on a tree
   needs water and sunshine
   can buy in a food store
   has vitamins
2. green colored
   people eat it
   vegetable
   needs water and sunshine
   can buy in a food store
   has vitamins
3. answers will vary
4. answers will vary

Page 9
1. answers will vary
2. C, E, C, E, E, C, E

Page 13
1. coins or money
2. fruit
3. things with stripes
4. things with four legs
5. things with wheels
6. pets or animals

Page 14
1. c
2. g
3. e
4. b
5. a
6. h
7. f
8. d

Page 15
food, animals, clothing

Page 16
rooms - kitchen, living room, bedroom, bathroom
shelters - house, apartment, trailer, tent
furniture - table, couch, chair, desk
jewelry - ring, necklace, bracelet, earrings
outdoor clothing - gloves, hat, scarf, boots
other clothing - shirt, skirt, dress, blouse

Page 17
baby animals - chick, calf, cub, colt
adult animals - cow, horse, bear, hen
animals - mammal, reptile, bird, fish
plants - flower, vine, tree, bush

Page 18
1. white rectangle
2. triangle
3. circle
4. apple
5. Carol
6. eraser
7. spoon
8. television
9. glove
10. twenty

Page 19
1. 10, 14, 90, 2, 8, 70, 20, 30, 18, 12, 50, 100
2. 10, 90, 45, 70, 20, 55, 30, 5, 50, 100
3. 45, 49, 30, 33
4. 10, 90, 70, 20, 30, 50, 100
5. 10, 14, 90, 45, 49, 70, 20, 55, 30, 18, 33, 12, 50
6. 45, 49, 9, 1, 55, 33, 5, 7

Page 23
1. F
2. F
3. O
4. O
5. F
6. O
7. F

Page 24
1. O
2. F
3. F
4. O
5. F
6. F
7. O
8. O
9. F
10. O
11. F
12. O
13. F
14. O

Page 25
1. F
2. O
3. O
4. F
5. F
6. O
7. O
8. F
9. F
10. O
11. O
12, 13, 14. answers will vary

Page 27
Giraffes are the most interesting animals in the zoo.
It is fun to watch them eat.
Their black tongues are funny looking!
They are beautiful animals.

Page 28
Will make wonderful pets.
The most exciting adventure story of the year!!
Reasonable price, good location, beautiful cozy rooms.
Our state needs a man like I.M. Honest. He will be the best senator ever to represent our state in Congress.
Best fried chicken in the U.S.A.
You'll love our chicken!

Page 31
1. dog barks
2. snowman began to melt.
3. Sarah cried
4. Michelle was worried
5. washed the sand castle away
6. got new dress all wet
7. Erik's bobber went down quickly
8. Paul was a big hero
9. made her drop her lunch

Page 32
1. e
2. j
3. g
4. b
5. c
6. h
7. d
8. f
9. a
10. i

Page 38
1. e
2. d
3. h
4. g
5. b
6. c
7. f
8. j
9. i
10. a

Page 39

1. -	2. -	3. +
4. +	5. -	6. +
7. +	8. -	9. +
10. -	11. +	12. +
13. -	14. -	15. +
16. -		

Page 40

1, 8, 6, 10, 2, 4, 9, 5, 7, 3

Page 42

1, 2, 5, 7

Page 43

Answers should follow existing patterns.

Page 44

Pattern should continue as given.

Page 46

1. bb, a, bb, ccc
2. black, white
3. black, gray, white
4. various answers possible, up, on
5. fruit, fruit, vegetable
6. girl's S-name, girl's L-name
7. boy's A-name, girl's L-name
8. skipping, look
9. 4, e, 5, 6
10. Wednesday, April
11. children, man

Page 47

1. ○ ● ● ● ○ ● ●   5. ⊙△⊙△

2. snap - clap   6. 10, 15, 5, 10

3. □○△   7. abc, xyz, abc

4. □ □ □ ■ □   8. 40, e, 50

Page 48

1. ♩ ♪ ♩ ♪
2. ♩ ♪ ♪ ♩
3. ♩ ♪ ♪ ♪
4. ♩ ♩ ♩ ♪
5. ♩ ♪ ♩ ♩

6. ■ ■ □ ■
7. ■ □ ■ ■
8. ■ □ □ ■
9. □ ■ □ ■
10. □ □ ■ ■

Page 49

1. 30, 35, 40   6. 10, 8, 6
2. 11, 13, 15   7. 28, 32, 36
3. 23, 4, 14   8. 70, 65, 60
4. F, F, G   9. F-name, G-name, H-name
5. 4, 40, 5

Page 50

1. 5, 7, 8, 9, 11
2. 8, 10, 12, 14
3. 11, 15, 17, 21
4. skip a letter; f, g, h, r
5. number in alphabet; e, g, j, z

Page 52

1. g	5. a
2. e	6. c
3. b	7. f
4. d	

Page 53

1. 2, 4, 1, 3   2. 4, 3, 1, 2
3. 2, 1, 4, 3   4. 2, 4, 3, 1
5. 4, 2, 3, 1
6. circle with two diagonals
7. larger rectangle
8. five-sided polygon

Page 54

1. ant, mouse, squirrel, horse, elephant
2. Alabama, Georgia, Indiana, Kansas, Wyoming
3. baby, pre-schooler, kindergartner, teenager, adult
4. March, April, May, June, August

Page 55

Answers may vary somewhat but should show a logical progression between items that come before and after.

Page 56

1. 45, 54, 405, 450, 504, 540
2. 1 inch, 1 foot, 1 yard, 2 yards, 1 mile
3. July 4, 1990; October 31, 1990; January 1, 1991; February 2, 1991
4. house, neighborhood, city, state, country
5. second, minute, hour, day, month, year

Page 57

1. 1, 3, 2   2. 3, 2, 1
3. 4, 1, 3, 2   4. 5, 1, 3, 2, 4

Page 58

bread, cheese, ham, lettuce, mayonnaise, onion, pickle, tomato
9, 3, 7, 1, 8, 2, 4, 5, 6

Page 59

5, 10, 2, 9, 7, 1, 3, 8, 4, 6

Page 60

1. 3, 2, 1   2. 3, 1, 2
3. 3, 2, 1   4. 2, 3, 1

Page 61

B3
B5
C9
A1
A2
B7 or C&
C10
B6
B4
C8

Page 62

A5
C7
A1
D10
B6
D12
A2
A3
C8
D11
A4
C9

Printed in the United States
by Baker & Taylor Publisher Services